At the Top

At the Top

This book will guide you to a lifetime of experiencing wealth and eternal bliss.

ERIKA GARCIA

Copyright © 2016 by Erika Garcia.

ISBN:	Softcover	978-1-5144-8971-0
	eBook	978-1-5144-8970-3

All rights reserved. No part of this book may be reproduced or transmitted in any form or by any means, electronic or mechanical, including photocopying, recording, or by any information storage and retrieval system, without permission in writing from the copyright owner.

Any people depicted in stock imagery provided by Thinkstock are models, and such images are being used for illustrative purposes only.
Certain stock imagery © Thinkstock.

Print information available on the last page.

Rev. date: 04/28/2016

To order additional copies of this book, contact:
Xlibris
1-888-795-4274
www.Xlibris.com
Orders@Xlibris.com
737860

CONTENTS

The Power is in You 1
Get to the Top 2
▼ Write Your Desires on Paper 3
▼ Have No Fear 4
▼ Your Thoughts Become Your Reality 5
▼ Change is Good 6
▼ Change Your Ways of Thinking 7
▼ Believe in You 8
▼ You Are the Genie 10
▼ Acceptance 11
▼ Your Thoughts are Signals Which Generate Results ... 12
▪ Energy 14
▼ The Brain 15
▼ Patience 17
▪ Highest Energy Level 19
▪ Never Become Discouraged 20
▼ Always Read 22
▼ Equations are Combinations 24
▼ Control Your Vibrations 25
▼ The Laws 26
▪ Focus 27
▼ Control Your Feelings 29
▼ Understand How Life Works 30

INSPIRATIONAL POEMS 33
Money 35
High 36
Seek and Find 37
Good Day 38
Tips to remember 39

Dear Reader's

Savannah, Georgia is where I was born and raised since December 16, 1986. As a child my favorite thing to do was read stories and create my own tales through experiences. Through my teenage years I discovered my niche for poetry. Blank page books were always the best gifts; my pleasure was filling all the pages with my poetic words. Literature has been my most liked subject during my schooling.

    The ultimate purpose of writing for my readers is to inspire and motivate each person. Focusing on clearing my mind in order to pin point exactly what my readers need revealed through my books that is be abundantly helpful is my purpose. At my most peaceful times during my days is when I am most energized which allows me to motivate my reader's through stories and poems, including useful vital information. Accomplishing the goal of informing my readers on how to experience eternal bliss and success is my message. Watch out for my new books in 2016.

Sincerely,

Erika A. Garcia, Author
March, 2016

After reading this book you will be able to physically change everything in your life into all things that you have been dreaming for all along.

Understand! Believe! Observe! Achieve!

The Power is in You

Associating with the rich success one's that has similar desires as yours in life, will help you get closer to your goals. Your focus- level is always important. Learning how to be happy right now at this every moment is vital to your ultimate bliss! You have to know what exactly you desire in life in order for it to come to me.

I learned life's secrets by observing those who inspire me in life. Knowledge is power! Believe and you shall receive, know it is possible and accept change so it can become true! Brain -food in knowledge! Books are power! Reading gives you knowledge. Always have a peaceful place rather it be a mental place or a physical place in case of frequency emergencies. First learn the basic sets to success and master my basics, to then channel your energy!

Get to the Top

The four levels of life are health, love, wealth, and relationships. Once you know how to control all four levels of your life nothing can stop you from reaching the top. Learning is the key. You have to be teachable in order to have a teachability- index.

Expand your heart and mind right now at this very moment in order to be as successful as you desire in life. Think of all your goals and dreams that you would love to make come true to accomplish a level of success. Think of these things as if they are around the corner and all you need now is the directions with the right steps on how exactly to get there. First believe in your dreams so that they feel real. Believe that you have already found out that you have accomplished your goals; therefore, it will become so.

▼ *Write Your Desires on Paper*

Start thinking of your life as if everything is already happened in your favor, therefore; when your desires physically come into your life it will not strike you by surprise! Important tools to use are blue ink and white paper for writing. Write down exactly what you desire for your life and think positive thought while you focus on these things in order for them to happen.

Make a list of all the goals you want to accomplish and put them in order with a time frame that will allow your brain to transmit your thoughts from seeing them on paper into a virtual reality this way the universe will know your desire. Your list is like the grocery list for your main dish. Everything will be your for your own choosing; it's like making a full course meal. Do you love to eat? Do you love to feel fulfilled in everything you do in life?

▼ *Have No Fear*

Move your energy to a positive level! Leave all those negative energies in the past. From now on every single one of your vibrations will control everything that happens in your life!

▼ *Your Thoughts Become Your Reality*

Always be willing for change in your life! Start a strong foundation for your life's desires by thinking what you want into existence! Make your list. Look at your dreams, read them every day, say they aloud as feel your energy flow through your entire body as if you have enter a new world and success has taken over your being.

▼Change is Good

Never think negative thought, they slow down the positive brainwaves that allows you to be exactly what you desire to be in your life! Love Self! Take Risk! Doing so is knowing that you can, therefore; those who do not do simply do not know that they are capable! Be open to letting new change happen in your life! Be willing to do the unthinkable n life in order to have productive change you want to happen in your life! Whatever you want in life you can have all it takes is the willingness to learn how!

▼Change Your Ways of Thinking

Always focus on learning from the best sources in order to be at a success level you desire for your life look for the right people to help inspire you! You make my own journey happen in life by thinking so, then knowing so, and believing, therefore; desires in life, they come true! After knowing how to think correctly in life, everything you want will flourish! Knowing so is the key that holds the power from within! This works, just simply apply yourself!

▼ Believe in You

Always use your brain it is capable of unimaginable things! Think! Think! Think! "I manifest what I want in life!" This is true. Read books in order to know how! This book holds the secrets to a successful life! Believe in order to not fail. Focus on exactly what you want in life. Write it down! Read! Learn! Focus! Find peace! These keys open up your brainwaves to allow the positive energy to flow correctly, thereafter; whatever you imagine for your life will come to you!

Dream so that they can come true! I fail at nothing there is a win in everything I do! Focus on it! Think it is so, Believe! Apply your positive energy in everything you do because the Law of Attraction is what forces the positive energy right back to you. This is a proven fact! The energy you use is from the feelings you may be experiencing at a particular moment.

In order to control your feelings, know how to use your energies correctly. The energy of shame will delay you from ever being productive in your goals towards success. If you have the energy of shame this simply means that you feel like things you have done in your life leaves you feeling not powerful enough as if the things you have accomplished are not as good as they should have been; therefore, these thoughts leave you in an energy field of shame. Always make yourself feel like you have done your best at everything you do in your life then you will never experience shame or the energy of gilt. Fear is also energy so control what you are thinking; it's that easy. Learn about your highest energy on page 11.

▼ *You Are the Genie*

If it is money that you want in your life then you can grant yourself money by focusing on prosperity in your life. Red on and learn how. Be specific with your own desires. Keep it real with yourself by all cost. The most ultimate sin is to deceive yourself by knowing one thing in your heart then saying or doing the opposite of the inner feeling which came from the heart. All you must learn how to do is dream and desire things you want in your life by focusing on those things. This allows your dreams, goals and desire to come true by your powerful demand.

The brain is the core element. Start training your brain to only accept and understand your positive thoughts. Always think positively. Say to you; "I can make all my dreams come true!" Read this information then utilize it. Learn this vital information then display your learning's through your growth throughout your life. You can reach results you want by simply learning the correct ways to think, which is called your teachability index, by learning, then allowing change to occur in your life you get what you what even through all the obstacles life may try to bring your way.

▼*Acceptance*

Acceptance is also energy. Use your energy of acceptance in order to move past the feeling of not wanting to let go of your old ways and things. 'To know is to believe and to have is to say so!' When bad things seem to happen, stay positive in order for the good to come back around your way, remember; it's the energy level you may be experiencing, therefore, change your frequency by thinking of your dreams and desire which should ultimately place you back in a calmer, happy, peaceful place.

Learning how to use this technique will block you from encountering all negative pathways. Never worry in life, always try to make yourself feel even more better through all good and bad things, life is whatever you make it out to be! Make all negative feelings turn positive with your thoughts Control your entire human-being then you can control your life. Find happy places you enjoy in order to have balance. Once you learn how to use your energy correctly then you will be able to influence the feelings of others in your life.

▼ *Your Thoughts are Signals Which Generate Results*

Your thoughts will give you exactly what you want; therefore, focus on only the positive in everything. Another important piece of information is to fix your thought pattern is to focus on not telling lies in life because when you tell your brain to change the truth you throw off the positive thoughts that were initially flowing to your brain, remember the thoughts are what makes things become true by the Law of Attraction. Speak what you want into your reality. Be honest at all times this makes life easier. Never allow you to feel bad in any situation, try finding the good things through positive thoughts. Say, "Even though I have no idea how, I know everything will work out find because I know things always work out in my favor!" Believe this when you say it! When you say words that you believe are true nothing in the universe can stop the positive energy from reaching positive energy, is a fact! Use words that make you feel amazing within. Learn to uplift yourself in a positive way with words.

Always care but not too much because sometimes you may not be able to realize the blessing at first through all the bad there is good within. The more and more you learn to live this lifestyle the easier it will be to conquer anything you desire. Expect it to happen, therefore, there are no surprises in life because didn't you know all along your success was coming even though time was not the element that held the power. You have the power because you believe it is so. Wealth, health, and happiness including all desires come by using positive energy from the Universe.

Knowing what you want then emotionally focusing on it, this allows you to virtually believe. Feel good at all times so your energy level stays the same in order to use your thoughts effectively to make things happen in your life by enjoying what you do every day to become successful.

Learn! Think! Know! Focus! Believe!

▪ *Energy*

The brain is a transmitter with extremely higher frequency. Everything is of atoms, which is an electron and protons rotating a nucleus. Energy holds the nucleus in place. Frequency is energy. Energy is vibrations. You can fill any place with my energy/ vibrations. A combination of atoms/ energy is what makes things appear to be different to the human eye. A combination of the correct vibrations is all it takes! Everything the eye can see is simply an energy vibration moving at different speeds.

You are creative and unique. Somehow you are always prospering to greater heights day after day. Knowing this helps you send that vibration into the universe activating the Law of Attraction. Energy equals frequency which equals humans, seaweed, clouds, etc. Frequency controls everything on the planet all you have to do is use your energy it's easy! You can transmit my energy to as high of a frequency as you desire by thinking. Understand your teachability index, be willing to always learn and except the change in life that is to come.

▼ The Brain

The brain power makes all things in life possible. Frequencies matter! Everyone knows about the Law of Gravity; well, the Law of Lift over powers the Law of Gravity. Even more powerful than them all is the Law of Attraction, which is that all vibrations that are the same attract. Therefore, use energy wisely to attract your desires into your life by believing. Remind yourself of the obvious things you desire in life. Always know that you are a winner even when it seems as if you actually lost at something; you still win because you took all the positive things with you, which then multiplied into even more positive energy giving you positive thoughts which in return made that lost a learning experience.

The brain is a powerful tool that allows dreams to come true! Use this information and change your life! There are a few major ways to enter the rich world and have anything you desire all you have to do is use a rich way of thinking. One of the most important things to remember is to eat properly. You must nourish your body. Your body is like your transportation to the rich world from the poor world, feed it accordingly. Feed your brain with brain-food like vital information from important sources, reading books, experiencing bliss through your life. Another thing to remember is to get rest. Resting is like recharging your physical battery inside of you. Without the proper rest your brain becomes chemically imbalanced.

Relax, there are many way to get rest without falling into a transit state of mind, which ultimately leaves you vulnerable at times. Too much sleep cripples the body over time. Keep your joints flexible and your muscles strong. The energy of courage will give you strength like a bull. Courage energy will allow you to do your most unimagined dreams. Courage is life changer energy.

▼ *Patience*

Be patient because wisdom is knowledge which all comes with a little time. Have no pride; the energy of pride is only what you believe in, although you can't change those beliefs. Travel into the rich state of mind in order to enter your rich world because it already exists. Having a high teachability index will allow you to learn through all things you experience in life. You must be willing to listen, learn, and observe, this is the way of life. Stop negative thinking in life in order to correct your thinking process. The thinking process is vital. Riches come from all the magnificent thoughts your brain has been transmitting your way.

The brain is what allows you to understand. The negative thinking will pattern will delay your natural smile. Smiling is like giving your brain a carwash. A smile reminds you to think of something happy. Once a positive though is signaled to your brain you are now on the pathway towards riches. Continue telling your negative thoughts positive things in order for your brain to transmit the positive desires you dream.

Allow all your positive brainwaves to intersect. When there is positive energy flowing through your thoughts at all times the wealth comes easily because your brain will not be blocking you from receiving the knowledge to conquer whatever you think of. Even what may seem like the worst situations will not disappoint you because all of your positive ways of thinking will not allow any negative energy to flow through to you.

▪Highest Energy Level

There are many different energy levels people may experience in life. Learn to use your energy of gratitude, this energy will allow new positive changes in your life. The highest energy level is joy. Once humans have reached their peak then nothing in the universe will hinder them from having anything their thoughts desire in their life. The riches people on Earth experience the sense of joy at some period in their life. This feeling allows them to never become ill-willed in any manner in their life.

A smile is a vital tool to use on the pathway to Energy of Joy. Remember, smiles are tools use them wisely. A smile can change the energy at any time. The brain gets a sense of calmness when the eyes send the vibrations from a smile to your frequency. A smile is a small gesture that can change a negative vibration into a good vibration every time.

The law of Attraction always will work even without s trying to use this law on purpose; it is scientifically proven it come from the Universe. Smiling often brings more positive energies your way. Smiling throughout the day keeps the negative energies away.

▪ *Never Become Discouraged*

Let the disappointments fly over your head as if they never happened at all; therefore, nothing will be able to take your energy by surprise. Surprises generally send glitches through your vibrations. Even once you become a millionaire, do not be surprised because you already knew it was going to happen all along, right? Because you think about how you desire your life to be all the time; therefore, you generated that millionaire energy to you. Just smile and accept the changes that are coming your way in order for your life to change.

Each morning, look in the mirror and smile. A smile can remind your brain to have positive energy flowing through your entire world. The energy you hold is extremely powerful because you possess a current of frequency that has connection to combinations of vibrations full of neurons.

Your energy allows you to be in control of the events that may happen in my life. By using your frequency correctly you can elevate to all things you desire in life. Anything can be mine for all my pleasure. Positive is the only way to be. Knowing how to remain positive at all times is the key.

The willingness to learn is something found from within each individual. Know that you are who you say you are; this simply thought pattern makes its true because you can made these thought turn into your reality by using my brainpower.

▼*Always Read*

Peace! Read! Learn! Listen! Observe! Teach! These are the main adjectives to remember to do in life in order to become successful. Find your peaceful place while you enjoy your given time here on Earth, because when you can mediate and focus on what it is that will make you feel satisfied in life, then ponder on your dreams in order to make those dreams you have a reality; you must be able to allow your brain to calm down from all the outside noises and disruptions throughout the lands.

The peaceful place you find will renew your soul with fresh thoughts to prosper in life. Your peaceful place(s) gives you extra room to prow all on your own in a unique way. Think positive thought and believe in yourself because knowing; then accepting the change that is about to happen in your life.

Most importantly, you must feel a sense of fulfillment and happiness now in life before your life changes because when you feel like you have already accomplished or achieved what you really desire it will be easier for the Law of Attraction to grant you the desires that are due to you. Positive brain frequency is the key. Just simply believe. Remember to smile through all types of energy waves that come your way.

A smile reminds your brain that everything will be all right. If you want to be successful then know you can be, this is the first step. If you know you are a winner then play a winner role. This tool allows your brain to believe your thoughts. What you are thinking is always vital to everything you will ever do in a successful life. Time does not play a factor for these things.

▼ Equations are Combinations

You are made of energy. Everything is energy. Kinetic energy is energy of motion. E= mc squared. Energy is time; time is energy; use time at your own speed. E= energy, m= mass, c= speed of light. Mass is a measurement of the quantity of matter. Matter is atoms. An atom is a nucleous surrounded by electrons and protons. Everything is made of atoms; human, plants, rocks, etc.

Everything needs a negative and positive charge and there' a source energy that holds it all together. Matter and energy are interchangeable. Energy is equaled to matter, multiplied by the speed of light, squared. Energy travels at light speed. Light speed is cosmic speed, which equals light.

▼*Control Your Vibrations*

Always remain calm even through times that may feel like war. Learn how to control your breathing; continue to breath, take small sometimes deep breaths in order to remain at the desired energy level of vibrations which make you successful. This is your ultimate focus and purpose. The brain is your own personal transmitter to anywhere.

Your brain holds an extremely high frequency, some can't even imagine. Everything is an atom, which is an electron and protons rotating a nucleous. Energy holds the nucleous in place. Frequency is energy. You can fill any place with your energy.

Energy is vibrations of combinations of atoms, the speed within atoms are what makes things appear to be different by the human eye. Everything the eyes see is simply an energy vibration. You can control anything with your energy at a high frequency. You can transmit your energy to as high of a frequency as you desire by using your brain. All it takes is understandings of these techniques. Your frequency matters.

▼ The Laws

We all know about the Law of Gravity. Well, the Law of Lift over powers the Law of Gravity. Even more powerful than them all is the Law of Attraction, which are all vibrations that are the same will attract to one another. Therefore; use energy wisely to attract your desires into your life by thinking of your dreams then believing they are true by allowing your brain frequency to pull your desires to you.

The Law of Attraction works rather the human brain knows about it or not. The Law of Attraction works unbeknownst to those who are unaware of the Law of Attraction itself. The brain transmits frequencies at all times. This is universal.

You will attract whatever it is you think about. Eliminate your fear and pain; therefore, the negative thoughts will not enter your pathway. Always focus on thoughts that make you feel better in life. Keep your emotions happy so your energy will continue to get stronger.

▪ *Focus*

Only think about what you want in life so those desires you want will come to you by your vibrations. There are two forms of energy potential energy and kinetic energy. Potential energy is any type of started energy. Kinetic energy is found in movement because kinetic energy is energy in motion.

Do not think about the time of the clock because once you start worrying about thing, your energy sends off that negative energy into the universe; which when delays your positive results from your initial positive energy you held in the first place. Focus and feel good about life; now, today.

Shout aloud your desires and jump for joy, feel your thoughts through your soul. Your have the power but only the gifted one's will discover exactly how to use their frequencies. You create what you want for your life simply by thinking of your desires.

Your wishes are at your command. Time is ill-relevant in the millionaire world as far as making what may seem like the most impossible desires a reality. You must define exactly what it is that you want in your life. What are your dreams and pleasures? Having fun with the things you do in life is extremely important.

Your energy is determined by in which you attract through your thoughts; therefore, remain at those feelings that only make you feel better than your current energy level. Ultimately, control your thoughts in return you control your world! Realize all things currently in your life that makes you feel a sense of happiness and fulfillment in order to accomplish your goals towards success, which comes to all positive vibrations through the Law of Attraction.

▼ *Control Your Feelings*

Try feeling good at all times; this vital. Even start using only words that are positive which makes you feel good. For example: "I am doing pretty well". "Everything will be fine." Words can determine your energies as well; rather the words you hear or say are positive or negative words.

Never use negatively energized words in your journey towards success. Avoid all negative pathways in order to bypass the delays. Negative energies vibrate at a low frequency and positive energy vibrates at a much higher frequency which allows your success to come to you. Be in bliss with your thoughts which allows your energy to remain positive. There is no radar in the world of success.

▼ *Understand How Life Works*

The nobodies are not going to want to read my books, only the somebodies in life will read my words because the nobodies never wanted to be a somebody from the beginning. Remember, readers are the leaders. Always expect your desires to happen; therefore, there are never any surprises because I knew it was going to happen anyways although time is no element that holds power.

The power is in you. Vision all your success in a long-term point of view; then, see your problems in a very short-term point of view, finally, use your thoughts in order to make your dreams come true.

Whatever you think in your mind will give off energy into the universe. Believe it is so; your wealth, health, happiness and so forth, by using positive energy while knowing what you want and emotionally focusing on those desires, which in returns allows you to believe in yourself.

Feel good at all times so your mental-energy level stays at a higher frequency in order to use your thoughts effectively to make things happen in your life, simply enjoy what you are doing. It does not matter how long you have been going through negative times, at that very moment you change your vibrations you change your life into positive vibrations. Remember energy is vibrations. The energy of love can change the entire world.

Learn! Think! Know! Focus! Believe!

INSPIRATIONAL POEMS

Money

Money, money, money
My mind can't stop thinking of what to do next
Each day keeping these numbers multiplying
to greater and greater heights
Although, I am over buying yachts and
Mansions with twenty plus rooms
I am at an elevation no airplane can reach
Money, money, money
You took me to Heaven and back
Again and again
Here I come doing unthinkable things
Nothing can stop me from doing
whatsoever my brain may dream
Watch me accomplish unimagined things

High

So high above it all
Nothing bothers me
Happy is the only way to be
Everything I desire is mine for the keeping
The ultraviolet white light guides my
eye sight towards all high things
Amazing full of grace
It is all the same
High above it all
From the bugs in the sand
To the elevating airplanes
A smile is what I keep on my face
It shields all the negative energy from coming my way
A combination of peace, love and happiness is all of me
My vibration raises my frequency high above it all
Nothing can move me

Seek and Find

Seek your desires in life
You shall find exactly what you are looking forward to
There is a danger sign covering your fontanelle
Because you are armed with the strength and
Power to find anything you please
Dream, Dream, Dream
All your desires can be
Believe in everything you do
Never put too much pressure on you
To know is to believe
Always think of the best things
Therefore, you will achieve
Simply seek and you will find
Whatever your thoughts generate from your mind

Good Day

Prospering in many ways
While trying to remain
Stay willing to change
Never stay the same
In order to gain a new prosperous way
Live blissfully
Laugh everyday

Tips to remember

Avoid negative thoughts; these thoughts can block you from the true frequency you desire to be at; stop all negative judgments because it limits all the positive things you are capable of pulling into your life -

Unless one changes his vibrations
he cannot feel the light -

He who believes in their inner light has everlasting blessings; and those who do not believe in their own light will not have eternal bliss, only their own self-destruction-

The light knows everything and everyone; furthermore, it has given me every pleasure that produces seeds which is found on all the soil of the Earth, every positive energy that enters me will be like food for me-

Let your emotions be without greed of possessions, be content generally in life. The light will never take off from oneself, nor will it led you the wrong way-

So, we all shall announce, "I am guided by the light; I do not fear, therefore, what can any person give me?"-

Do not believe in any diagnoses of sicknesses because
the positive energy is in your being. Remain happy.
You are your own blessings, not with energies that have
not past participle of those whom have been blessed-

Every living thing is born with the intent to survive,
all living things have instinct like intuitions; so,
we seek the light in order to find the right path-

Right and wrong, positive and negative, these energies
do not attract; so, always observe and learn-

Let your thoughts speak what you want
into your life from the universe –

Change your energy in order to change your life –

Once you have connected with your oneness
then proceed to ask the Universe questions the
answers will show up in your life physically. –

Always remind yourself of how grateful
and thankful you are every day -